Hanging Dog Creek

❧

Mary Ricketson

FUTURECYCLE PRESS

www.futurecycle.org

Published by FutureCycle Press
Lexington, Kentucky, USA

ISBN 978-1-938853-72-2

Dedicated to my son, Lee

and to the memory of my parents
Luke and Marian Peavey

In appreciation of Southern Appalachian creeks, gardens,
and mountains that heal and inspire me

In grateful and loving appreciation of my teachers,
Nancy Simpson MFA and Gene Hirsch MD

Contents

III

Moonlight on Creek Rock

IV

Indigo Bunting in Flight

Acknowledgments

I

Feet Wet in Dew

Telegram

A bird comes to visit
every morning
at my bedroom window.
I sip coffee, slowly wake.

Black and white chickadee
sings in shape-notes,
colorful like autumn leaves
down the valley view.

Perched on a power line,
puffed up for warmth,
his tail twitters, his song an opera.
Every burst of joy, every measure of song
seems a message in a language I don't know.

Suddenly he darts at the window.
Two or three slams at the unyielding glass,
then he's back, settled on his wire.
I shudder. Birds die this way.

But he returns every day
uninjured, undaunted,
belts out his melody.

Walnut

Suddenly I remember
life is hard.

One walnut tree stands
at the end of my field.
Forty years I watch. It never wanders,
never moves, only sheds its leaves,
drops its weakest branches
when storms rage through the cove.

What is a woman,
but a tree that walks around?
Storms and seasons leave scars
on ripened beauty,
carve hearts in the bark
where mysteries of strength lie
in the eyes of each beholder.

No decision diverts the tree.
A tree does not worry about its fate.

At Home on Hanging Dog Creek

Sun shines on purple
phlox and chigger weed.
Ticks hide in tall bush.
Dogs collect them only
to occupy my idle after-supper
porch-setting time.

Rhododendron hells
and dog hobble claimed
some ancient bear dog.
He didn't make it home
one blue-skied autumn hunt.
Indians, time out of mind,
called this place Hanging Dog Creek.

Water rushes
over big grey rocks,
disturbs fallen sticks,
collects used-up roots and time,
creates cover for young trout.
Sounds carry my mind down-creek.

Full moon finally peeks
over Flea Mountain.
My thoughts hang between
sounds of bullfrog calls.

Garden

Hot sun beats upon beads
of sweat rolling down my head.
Shards of dirt fall
from my feet and fingers.
From toil and pleasure,
deep in blackest earth,
come roots of finest food.
From sweat and dirt
comes a cleansing,
ceremony that binds my
name to this land.

Lost in the Roar of Big Santeetlah

I cross a wooden bridge.
A stand of dark red trillium
waits for my attention.
White violets and crested dwarf iris
sit quietly at trail's edge. Birdsong begins.
Butterflies dance. Jack in the Pulpit presides.
River birch, pine and poplar stand tall.
Rippling water stills my thoughts.
I can taste the wind.

Soon pink lady slipper will bloom,
then purple rhododendron.
I know every season at this forest.

I fell in love here long ago,
found comfort on this path,
met parts of me I did not know,
told secrets never spoken.
Trees made promises,
then asked for mine.
I fill myself with peace and hope when I am here,
then give it all away when I am gone.

Manifesto

My body knew
before my mind
made thoughts,
before my voice
found words.

Make peace with loss.
Make friends with change.

A candle flickers.
Blue light drowns
in its own flame.
Secret shards
of hope surrender.

Let me live
where crystal-clear creeks
slither over small stones,
ripple over rugged rocks,
slide through the smooth,
and rain and tears are welcome
as sunlight and laughter.

Where birth and death
run the same river bed,
I run my life.

Fireflies

Twinkling lights in early evening
call my name, invite me out.
I walk the lane to settle myself
from a long day.

A million tiny glimmers of joy
draw me farther down the gravel
road and around the curve,
past horses and houses
and gnarled locust fences.

Sparkles of the ancient insect
slip me back to a faerie ring
where magic and sacred
have been one word.

When I was four, a wise old woman
took me to a child-place, a fairyland.
Billions of tiny lights sparkled on the trees.

A little older, I reached out,
caught a glowing lightning bug,
drawn by the spirit of its glimmer.
A hundred more quickly passed me by.

Now I am content to gaze
into the flickering mystery.

Star Dance

It was as if I was a giddy young girl
in the antebellum South, gone home
to tell her Nanny all about the evening
that made time stand still and the world glow
with golden red-hot flames on a starry night.

I danced with a man that night.
Three times we twirled and swirled,
flew into the stars.

His eyes held the light of Orion.
I could not look away. He smiled.
Somehow he knew my name.

Still I thought it was just a moment.
But as I turned to exit,
there in the doorway he stood.

I don't remember driving home.
I'm sure I rode on the tail of a shooting star.
I left the mail, left the dishes, left the messages.
I sat in my old wooden swing by the giant poplar.

Venus was like a comet that night.
A whippoorwill called. Later an owl flew past.
A few young cherry trees made a ring,
waltzed in the evening breeze.
Fairies danced in my garden, among basil and sage.

Sunday, Seven A.M.

The waning moon
looked graceful
in the eastern sky.
I hardly felt the frigid
wind as I collected wood
to start my parlor fire.

And then the moon
slipped aside, replaced
by red and pink clouds
presiding over last night's
yet untrodden snow.

In a moment it was over.
I stepped inside, arms full of logs.
But I was warmed before
the fire warmed the room.

Building the House on Hanging Dog Creek

We were hippies then,
disillusioned by the American dream.
Moving back to the land,

we ignored the best jobs,
chose Appalachia for beauty.
We set out to build a home
with our own hands,
grow food, create a self-sufficient life.

Saving for years, finally it was time
to frame, roof, wire and plumb.
Every detail is still embedded in my mind:
Mark with batter boards.
Dig, level, set joists, lay floor, raise walls.
Become expert with hammer and nail.

An old house provided salvage oak,
glass, and doors. We tore it down.
Pulling nails, sorting wood
taught me patience I had not planned to learn.
We built our doors and windows in a class,
learned the tools, sanded for hours.

I remember dancing through the house,
both stories standing tall and straight.

Just an Old Fashioned Love Song

Squishing Japanese beetles
along rows of blueberries,
you down one row, me another,
we walk through common
garden chores and tasks.

These demons of the garden
stake claim to our bushes,
devastate the crop.
Eradication is what we're after,
one beetle at a time.

Japanese beetles are too sophisticated
to succumb to common cures.
At first sight of the creepy little bug,
we police the rows, armed with fingers,
mason jar and lid.
Squish, plop. Squish, plop.

Along my watch, beetle decimation in progress,
I squish remains of my own old armor.
Battle done, prize won.

Living with Nature

Warm from the sun
but still long-sleeved,
I survey the early garden:
faded yellow daffodils,
budding azaleas in purple,
mounds of deep-green thyme
and oregano ready to eat.
I inhale one easy breath
of contentment,
then a sudden gasp.

A dead bluebird
lies in a tuft of green grass,
both my dog and my cat
near enough to blame.
They do not move.

Six eggs still fill
the unguarded nest.

Toddler at Home

You tricked me,
offered a Coco Puff,
really a morsel of dog food.
I can still hear your laugh,
full-bodied, giddy, wide open,
when I spit it out.

An elfin fairy,
imp untamed,
your unfettered life
incited an uprising
against the sixteen-year quiet
of our small house in the woods.

I remember the time
you asked me
for a little brother.
It was the first time
I could not supply
your heart's desire.

Alacrity

"Let's go with alacrity!"
you hollered to me.

Word you learned
on Monday night football.

I had to ask you precisely
what it means.

"Moving on with great speed,"
you answered to me.

Christmas comes
soon for us this year.

The puppy I gave to you as a toddler
is already an aging old pooch.

Now your clothes must
be only the latest in fashion.

Your hair is just right
and your shoes are untied.

I don't know the answers to all
of your homework today.

The nest of our home grows smaller
as the world widens for you.

Yesterday a babe, you
sat crooked in my arm.

Today you stand tall.
You come up to my nose.

The time we spend eating
cookies is priceless to me.

Your life passes by me
with too much alacrity.

Eight Miles to Home

The first curve swerves me across two bridges.
I pass a lone stand of neighborhood houses,
freshly mowed grass, stuffed mailboxes,
flower beds, and benches under shade trees
where children romp and run.

Now I twist and turn along a two-lane strip.
Three more hairpin turns, I pass a store
that sells a last-chance bit of everything.
I glance at my gas gauge; no need to stop today.

Another sharp turn speeds me on,
more trees than buildings now.
I smile at an ornate tin roof to my right,
held up by more house than not.
I remember an old man there.
His chickens ran loose in the house.
I don't know how long he's been gone.

A hundred and one curves
carve this road from town to my place.
A familiar landscape waits around the next curl.
I take a breath and blink my eyes,
slow down from thirty-five to twenty-five.
A hawk flies by.

Green mountains break the horizon,
reach out to me in grand caress,
still my thoughts, rhythm my mind.
My mountain stands
as dominion of peace in this valley.

Whispers of whippoorwills
once called me here.
Now a hundred and one curves
mother me all the way home.

Flight

A bird came into my house today,
flew around, bumping into windows
and walls, fretted about,
held its mouth open,
waiting for food I think.

Someone will die.
That's what the old timers
say if a bird
enters your home.
Someone of yours
is what they mean.

My mind goes
to one who fights for life,
then to one who waits to die,
then the young one driving
the roads today, the one with life
ahead. Spare him, I pray,
as though I have a clue
what is best.

II

Mountain Laurel in Bloom

Old Brown Box

An ancient womanly ritual
calls me to my kitchen,
to a ragged brown box,
family recipes scribbled
by hand, careful instructions

for holiday meals and treats
made by my mother,
her mother, all the mothers.

Details step by step,
my mama's words
offer one encouraging note:
You will remember this when you begin.

With wooden spoon I stir the beloved mixture
in her chipped blue bowl.
I surprise myself with tears.

Jack Hall Remembered

Take a block of wood,
carve away everything
that don't look like
a squirrel, Jack told me,
but wait, use my pocket
knife, not that hog sticker
you brought. Here, I'll fix
you one ear. Watch, then you
carve the other'n.
Now that looks good.
See how the grain comes
out in that cherry wood.

Talk of vinegar pie
and tales of straightenin
nails to build his house.
Great whittler kept a slight smile,
a steady blue-eyed gaze.

Now sand him real good,
first with eighty grit,
down to double ought,
smooth as glass. That's it.
Now his eyes. Make the left
one first, so your hand
don't cover up when you do
the right. Now that's a good
squirrel. Paint it with Deft
and then you're done.

Ten years sayin' *Ain't*
you ever gonna
graduate this class?

Jack Hall was a master woodcarver,
teacher, and member of the Brasstown Carvers,
John C. Campbell Folk School

Back to the Campfire

This foggy morning takes me back
to campfires and tents. Smoky Mountain
trails, me and my pack, I found home for the night
by a clear running stream and foraged dry wood.

Evening flames lasted late, created comfort
that set up residence and never left me.
A well-stoked fire kept embers hot till dawn
when I rubbed my eyes, tripped through the flap,
found my poking stick, and built up the fire.

Coffee lasts a long time when you set your cup
on a hot rock smack in the fire. Mist-filled mornings
lasted long as I reviewed yesterday's hike
and thought toward today's trail.
Water on my face never felt so cold.
Bacon and eggs never tasted so good.

In time I packed my gear and bid goodbye
to trees that felt familiar after only one night,
but the mist that enveloped me stayed,
acquainted me with peacefulness.

Unspoken

This land was tended long and nurtured well.
When I breathe the air around this place,
I inhale endurance, love and care
grown from hearts that labored and laughed
season after season, year after year.

No marks grade each human word
spoken or unspoken, deeds done or left undone,
just a sense that life was lived for one more day.

When I don't know what to do,
I sit and breathe and I believe
that days gone by can nurture times to come.

I Knew

I would give
my last breath,
my last zest for life
to your father
rather than keep
it for myself.

I saw myself
in a mirror
dying, no disease
but a broken heart.
I saw myself
in the world,
jealous of anyone
having a happy time.

I knew love better
than most married people.
I had a best friend
who knew me like
no one ever had.
I had a partner
who made life happen.
That's how it used to be
before the black dog
moved in to stay.

I had a love that laughed
at trouble, made the sun
shine on a rainy day.
My love brought birds
and flowers, trickling
brooks and mountaintops.

I saw him shrink away
so I held him closer.
He cried in the corner
so I kissed him more.
He failed at work
so I worked harder.

Now, holding a memory
like a firefly closed in my hand,
a time comes when I know
I've held it long enough.
I open my hand.

Wet Exit

Finally my chance came in a rush.
Borrowed boat and supplies,
teacher in tow, I headed to white water,
class one rapids of the Tellico River.
Rhododendron blooms flanked the bank.

I had to learn to turn over, me inside
the kayak, release a rubber skirt
from the edges, exit the boat underwater,
and come up for air before drowning.

Three times I tried. Three times my mind
left my body. Both my arms froze up,
legs flailing in desperation.
Fears of a lifetime shot
through my mind in one second.
I knew I would drown.
I grabbed at the legs of my buddy,
a man I met only minutes before,
a man who did not foresee need for a rescue.

My run on the river promised
a wild carefree day, a day
free from worries and stress.
I ignored the irony. I found safety
in the hands of a stranger.

Finally I did it, paddled and laughed
my way downstream, one new buddy
or another nearby for the save.
One high-stress jaunt, first and last,
one less item on my bucket list.

Born to Walk

In the dark
hallways where ghosts
of ages lurk, my history
hides and waits.

I prepare myself.
No backpack. No tent.
Only water for the washing.

I was born to walk
where angels do not live,
where invisible demons
lie in wait, pretend to love.

Before I die
my journey will cut down
ancient icons of a time
when eyes were closed
and memories were zipped shut.

What else is there to do?
I must hike a trail
too dark for trees,
too narrow for two.

Make Myself Talk

Lured into two minutes of hell,
I push to get a word out clearly.
First the tension: throat, lips, chest.
Then the freeze: mouth stuck, immobile.
Frantic, my eyes blink, face contorts.
My hands wave erratically.
I am a freak.

On the school bus children
ask why I talk funny.
On the playground they tease,
mimic my stutters, mock
while I struggle to speak.

In high school I am afraid to talk,
know the answers, never raise my hand.
Embarrassment swarms around me
like a mass of mosquitoes in summer.
Bitten, swelled up in welts,
I know no one else like me.

I sit by friends,
make sure I am a good friend,
need friends to help me talk.

I try to be mute,
miss dessert, dates, jobs
by not speaking. I get tired.
Finally I give up on giving up.

Courage grows from sliver to seed.
I make myself face people,
make myself talk.

Secret Scars

She is smitten
by his first touch.
Already she belongs to him.

Blindfolded,
she does not see
what she surrenders.
His affection feels honest
and secure.
But what seems sincere
might be façade.

She speculates,
clouded cause and effect.
Euphoria drifts in like a spell.
She is duped, drugged,
feels soothed, reassured,
smothered in the attentive arms
of his caress.

She finds comfort
where comfort
was when life was crazy,
when all the grown-ups
wore blindfolds
and no mother's child
could comprehend
the cunning touch
of older hands.

Pick Flowers

Let me get away
from what is right,
what is wrong,
who needs what
and what needs me.

Let me breathe some air,
feel the rain on my face,
and bask in the smell
of fresh-cut grass.

Let me roam the forest
where trees much taller
than me stand straight,
never stray, and stay
right where they need to be,
never entertaining
one single doubt.

Let the wind move me
against my will,
put my power
into perspective.

Let me walk these fields
until grass teaches me
how to grow.

Community Men

Other women's men
came to build
my deck, make
me safe from falling
through cracks
formed from neglect,
derelict disregard
and outright obstinance.

I didn't know
how bad it was
till other women's men
repaired and rebuilt
with wooden planks
and nails of steel.

Buzzing saws and bits of dust
generated my resolve
to remodel a future
from my past.

Other women's men
ate my soup
when work was done.
No words were spoken
about the past,
but we all declared it done.

Salvage

It was the lumber that called me
to the barn. Years and years of storage
blocked my way.

I found the plastic tubing we used for a level,
building the foundation of our house.
Back then it was clear, just like our life.
Now it's black from ages of disuse.

Fly-fishing line appeared, then our tent
that housed us along the trails of our youth.
A dibbling bag for planting and a shearing knife
to trim the Christmas tree crop showed up in one corner.
Six rusted hand saws hung on the wall
along with drill bits, carving tools,
and a broken whetstone.
Once we were fervent in our farming chores.

Little boy clothes
and Teenage Mutant Ninja Turtles,
matchbox cars, and Legos.

I found my life, right where I left it,
before we let the wood shop go to hell,
before the barn became a storage shed.
I swept up dirt, leaves, nails and screws.

Now I clean up the cobwebs of my life.
I don't go near the crib we built
when I was pregnant. I ignore the bed
that used to be ours.
I will not look you up
to tell you what I've done today.

III

Moonlight on Creek Rock

Lunar Magic

Watch this winter wolf moon.
Here, grab a coat, sit with me on my deck.
Sky colors—pink, yellow, violet—
light up bright beneath this lunar face.

Watch, spellbound next to me,
quiet, no distraction. There is power
in the moon. Look how the stars know their place,
let the moon howl at center stage.
Full, brilliant light rules.
Emotion speaks. Listen.
Watch till clouds cover the face of the moon.

The Counselor

Like a willow,
I change with the seasons.
I bend with gusts of wind.
Women and men seek rest
and comfort in my shade.

I know the secrets of many.
I know their clandestine loves,
lies, truths, and bewilderment.

I know more of the angst
and less of the pleasures
of more lives than I can count.

I know the fears of many.
I help them carry building
stones and mortar of hope.

I walk through fire with some,
dive into undertow with others,
hoist a hand.

I have given my last drop
to a starving soul.
Life insists on change.
Torrents of tears resist.

I bend.
I listen to secret
whispers of winds.

Blind bridges of help and hope
are what I know will save this world.

Sleepless

I wonder
why the night
wakes no one
else but me.

I wear the world
by day; words
slip through,
up one side,
down the other.
Chores do me,
unless I do them.
Wishes and wants
appear as warp and woof,
in color and black and white.

I make notes.
I read awhile,
file my fingernails,
and listen to music.

Sets of wooden stairs
climb me up,
slide me into bed.
Toasty, comfy, cozy,
I close my eyes
while every tired muscle
in me wakes and waits.

Counsel for Myself

I am a place
where people
pilgrimage
the mysteries
of their lives.

I belong to adventure.
I am an anthropology
of psychic alterations
and effervescent lust
looking for life illuminated.

When I feel a storm
coming on,
I pick bouquets
of daisies before
it is too late.

I want a silver platter,
exquisite in design,
nothing but the best,
big as my arms can hold.

Bring it to me.
I need to unload my cauldron
of life-and-death responsibilities,
people with grief and sorrow
who find a home with me.

I need a rest from worry
and surveillance. If I could
free my arms from all I hold,

I would hold myself,
rock myself, dance
until an angel comes
and sings me softly into sleep.

Mother

You endowed me with sewing,
colors that go together,
and hope beyond hope.
Your obsessive optimism
tied our life together,
serged rough edges
into a decorative seam.

I still miss you
in the tears beneath my tears.

A thousand times I paced
my wooded path
the night before your death.
I heard the banshee cry.
Your dying days became my relief.
I craved your approval.
Giving up spiraled my completion.

Pruning Time

I've never done this before,
never cut out unneeded parts.
These thirty-year blueberry plants,
nine feet high, are too tall
to pick without a ladder,
too dense and matted for sun
to reach every limb.

I have to do this, sacrifice the size
of these mother bushes,
improve the yield, make the harvest.
I have to discard part of the last many years.

Hand clippers, long-handled loppers,
and a good eye at my command,
I plunder through a maze of dormant limbs.
Prune no more than one third of each bush,
I repeat like a mantra,
the only thing I know for sure,
then circle each one four times,
looking for what I have missed.

Often surprised or confused,
something comes clear.
I've always done this,
cut out parts of life
that no longer function.

Grief

Great seeds of anguish
ambush my blood and breath,
incite rebellion in thoughts
normally sane, logical, rational.
I need the garden more than it needs me.

Weeds I pull withstand torment,
receive my fury,
soak up poison, purify my heart.

Dark brown topsoil crumbles
at my hand, opens space,
receives my waste
without reprimand.
Soft particles of earth compost
my thoughts.

Ritual

Let this land work its magic.
Listen as one bird calls to another.
Let their song strum my strings,
send a dream to the tallest treetop.

Walk the road, walk the field,
walk the lane that leads toward home.
Pass by unsaddled horses, long-eared mules,
a neighbor's old plank barn
and the remains of my old chicken coop.

Stop, pick flowers with one hand,
pet the dog with the other,
tug on vines and brambles,
piddle with things that never ever get finished,
observe tufts of grass too tough to trample down.
Feel the moist earth give with every step.

Appalachian Gold

Zero degrees all night long,
water faucets quit at 2 a.m.
Drip, drop, drip, then nothing.

I pace the floors, sort
possibilities for the easy fix,
but call the plumber in the morning,
add my name to a four-day list.

An army of jugs, pots, pitchers and cans
of water line my counters and floors,
sentries for snowbound waterless infinity.

Snow is magical and mystical
till trouble ruffles its beauty.
I crave my normal life.
Now I see how ancient man
found deity in the sun.
It looks like Appalachian gold.

Embrace

Down on Dockery Creek
the climbing tree transforms in fall,
rough brown bark a background
for silks and linens of gold,
green, red, and orange.

Shades of scarlet invite
me up to a familiar nook
three branches above ground.
I steady myself,
embraced in immense arms
while I gaze out to a world
that does not know I'm here.

Hidden away, my mind ferments
like berries into fine wine,
restores accord.

This tree has known me forever,
has held me strong.

Evening Spell

In the quiet stillness I wait,
sit without thoughts or words.
I do not move.

Out on this porch I will not remember
what chores need doing inside the house.
Frogs croak in the distance,
harmonize with crickets.
A slight breeze brushes my face.
My potatoes in the field are laid by,
take care of themselves.
Nothing needs me now.

IV

Indigo Bunting in Flight

To My Only Child

The moon was full the night before,
lighting my steps as I walked and walked,
movement to invite you out of me.

What would I do
without frogs croaking
in the pond after dusk,
without fireflies lighting
the evening sky in June?

I was afraid and unafraid.
You took your time, always your own pace
right from the start.

What would I do without
corn to hoe, greens to cook
and berries to pick?

Suddenly there you were, crooked in my arm.
Your eyes met mine for the first time.
I promised to keep you safe and help you grow.

What would I do without a grown son
to telephone at night, and his grandmother to brag to after that?

It was hot the day you were born.
The world was ripe with food fresh-grown
and bluebirds sang to welcome the boy
and the mountains echoed joy and wild abandon.

Tonight is the eve of my only child's birthday.
He is three thousand miles away, filled with today.
Here on the deck where it's quiet, my mind travels.
What would I do without these trees
who hear my confession every night?

Backstitch

My mother's sewing machine stares at me.
Shiny black body in mahogany dress,
it commands honor, respect, almost adoration.

Slowly I cleanse a thick layer of dust from its entire surface.
I open the case, set a spool of thread in place.
I enjoy the filament between my fingers as I cross left,
down the essential eyelets exactly as I was taught.
I test a row of perfect black stitches on red.
I backstitch in time.

I am four years old.
I am allowed to cut threads and watch,
sitting on a stool left of my mother.

I am six.
I can thread the machine. I can pin pattern to fabric,
watch Mother cut. I am mesmerized by the needle
going in and out, latching the bobbin thread,
motor running fast and furious.
I can take the pins out of her perfect seams.
I want to be older. I sew doll clothes on a toy machine.

I am eight.
I sew my first seams, sitting in front of my mother,
my hands on her hands. Then my fingers are on the cloth,
near the needle as it runs. Her fingers are close to mine.
Soon I am permitted to sit on the stool alone,
make the magic myself as the machine hums along.

I am sixteen. I model my own creations.
I am nineteen. I have a sewing machine of my own.
I earn money mending and making outfits.

I grow older. I sew skirts, dresses, shirts, coats, vests,
curtains, even tablecloths with napkins to match.
I visit, show off my best pieces.
At the end, my mother's machine is closed.

Best of Everything

The way he smiled,
reached for my hand,
and mouthed *Good to see you*
the last time I saw him conscious
will never leave my heart.

The way he gobbled down
an ice cream bar the last time
he ate will never cease to amuse me.

The way he jiggled his legs and feet
after hip surgery, just to gain some strength,
and the way he teetered and struggled
into a chair after back surgery
will never leave my memory.

The way he made friends
with every nurse and doctor
and told them *Best of everything*
will always make me smile.

His words, *I don't have to live all that long,*
will always give me courage.

The time he told me
You must be the best mother in the world,
going by how good Lee is doing,
is already engraved in stone for me.
I knew it was our last talk.

I will remember all these things forever,
my lingering look at Luke's last days.
But the day he did not know
I was his daughter
is already fading away.

Absent

Those old live oaks look like battered women now.
I remember them draped in fine Spanish moss,
branches hanging to the ground,
grand curtsy to all comers by.
Welcome home to Biloxi, one always said
in a long southern drawl,
take off your shoes, feel the sand between your toes,
watch the evening sun sink down into the Gulf.
I obeyed without hesitance,
then sank my teeth into hush puppies,
steamed shrimp, and stuffed flounder.
Later I'd wile away the hours with Daddy,
he in one rocker and me in the other,
no particular things to say.

Everything changed when a great storm fisted up,
beat the living daylights
out of every tree along the coastal edge.
Naked and blown, branches broke to the stub.
Only raw strength and basic beauty remains
in the absence of Spanish moss.

Today, after the funeral,
a few gulls whisper as the tide comes in.
A sad refrain overshadows my own grief.
My live oaks will survive.
In time their limbs will reach out
to hug me when I come back.
But the Spanish moss is gone,
and Daddy's chair is empty.

At Joyce Kilmer Memorial Forest

Rhododendron leaves and white pine
boughs greened the scene,
though oaks and poplars were bare.
I brought my cares with me
to walk through the virgin forest.
I hoped to lose the heavy load along
some wild path in Kilmer's place,
enchanted with poetry and trees.

A midday fog hid
all the sun. It tried to rain.
The day was somber. So was I.
I found a place called Naked Ground,
a bottomland where Big Santeetlah flowed.

I sat on a dark cold rock
to watch white-capped ruffles
roll and gurgle in an ancient stream.

A symphony of water
rushed over rocks,
syncopated my thoughts,
lulled my cares
into some quiet corner,
and whispered,
"There, there, now go to sleep."

The sun peeked out.
I got up slowly,
hoping Big Santeetlah
would send a dream
to my sleeping cares,
change their tune
before they wakened.

My Living Room

Laughter fills the room.
Friends came yesterday,
willing hands, strong shoulders,
moved furniture, remade my home.
Pockets of joy still linger in every corner.

Another man is gone, took his tool belt
and his manly know-how, rolled down his sleeves
in after-work fashion, put the key in the silver car,
and drove down the driveway one last time.

I fix the plumbing with borrowed cans
of cleaner and glue. I wash dishes, load laundry,
leave grass unmowed and weeds unpulled.

I walk back to my living room
and set an amber candelabra on my glass table,
all polished up without a smudge.
An unexpected smile finds my face,
flirts and wants to play.
I recognize a whimsy, a bounce in my step,
an old melody that is mine.
I marvel at my own thrill. Laughter fills the room.

First Frost

Still dark, morning drags me
out of my cozy bed.
One foot, then another, slides
into thinly lined slippers,
braves the newfound cold,
trots me downstairs to the kitchen.

I ignore last night's dishes,
make coffee, check e-mail
while the caffeine drips
through dark brown grounds.

Don't turn on the heat so soon,
a voice from my checkbook pleads.
*Don't build a fire till the chimney
sweep comes,* a voice from my head warns.

I grab my steaming mug, climb back upstairs,
snuggle back under covers alone,
coffee and a good book to warm me
till sunshine comes over the mountain.

Canine Coach

Rest by the fire in winter,
she shows me.
But go outside to play
when the sun comes out and shines.

Sniff before you eat,
bark at troublemakers,
growl at suspicious ones.
Drink only in protected areas.

Have no patience
for dogs who pick fights,
bite, or intimidate.

Nuzzle with care.
Use your muzzle,
insist to lick and pet
when someone grieves and cries.

Expect to be petted,
cooed with tender scratching,
loved on as if nothing else matters.

The Arrival

My son sleeps outside on the upper deck
of a freshly rented student apartment
pretending comfort on a ten-dollar couch.
I slip through a sliding door and sit
nearby on a folding chair, coffee in hand,
careful not to wake him.
I am visitor to a life that is not mine.
Linked by lines of blood
and unbending care, I pilgrimage to his place
of budding life and endless study.

I take his bed, change my clock,
fly the skies, see the sights.
I bring cookies from home,
christen this abode with familiar
scents and savory. This is my stamp
of approval, blessing his choices.

Midsummer Night

Evening light wells up
soft and tranquil.
The mystic creek flows forever
over frigid rocks.
A nightly symphony
of crickets and running water
begins when twilight matures.
Near the end of dusk
fireflies flicker,
welcome dark
as day is done.
A whippoorwill calls.
I go inside.

Tonight, near midnight,
a loneliness wells up
inside the walls
and under the floor.
Emptiness prevails.
Birds don't sing.
Prayers seem unheard.
Only a book
can fill the void.

I wait for clarity,
conjure contentment
more than exuberance,
and I wait for morning.

Done In

Weeds take over.
Grass grows
amid mint stalks,
zinnia, and hollyhock.
Air breathes heavy
after sunshine
displaces the early mist.
Morning glory vines
declare ambush against
blueberries and okra.
Squash and beans are gone,
claimed by the dank
dog days of late summer.
Potatoes are laid by.
Empty corn stalks,
slashed at the base,
cover the garden floor.
Tomatoes still thrive red
among the weeds,
vines bent by heavy fruit
in an untended space.
Out front,
one violet gladiola
rises above the mess.

Stones at Sunset

I mow around each blueberry bush,
check for fungus, culprit that stole
my crop last year. Later I'll be back,
pull out persistent inner weeds.
Plump green berries
inform me without speaking,
This could be a good year.

By fluke I found this path,
grew beyond my plans.
Familiar now, I did not grow up this way.
Fate steered me in different directions.
My hands encourage these berries
to give sustenance and health.

My after-supper walk
rhythms my thoughts, calms my mind.
White blooms of blackberries
lead the way, then bursts of daisies
cluster under locust and barbed wire fence.
Three horses almost say hello.

I spy a neighbor's stone wall,
grey and brown random rocks
dug from a garden one by one,
stacked with no mortar, held together
only by weight and gravity.
In this light, accidental patterns of stones
resemble the chance routine of my life.
Will gravity hold me up so well?

I Hear the River Call My Name

Hiawassee River winds
where I go to rest my mind
from a hard day of work.
I make my way down to the river.
I walk along grassy banks.

I gaze at ripples.
Granite boulders grip my mind.
I marvel at their strength.
Branches, leaves, and bits
of trash float downstream.

A steady current gentles
through my mind.
A rush of water splashes
up against an edge of rich black dirt
and runs crystal clear.

Dark ripples tear
through the middle.
My raucous thoughts hide
like wild trout hide in the deep.

I slow my pace.
Sounds of running water
rhythm through my thoughts.
I hear the river call my name,
and I know what to do.
One by one, I cast my burdens
and watch them float downstream.

At Leatherwood Falls

Lost in a world
without words,
I linger on a ledge
between brashly
falling waters,

waiting for wind
to whisper.

I am delicate now,
almost fragile,
like a fine antique
with exquisite patina
that comes only with age.

I wear a *handle with care* label
reserved for rare or expensive goods.
I require time, quiet, and attention
to understand my complexity.

I aim to become a prism
of many facets, light shining,
refracted on each surface,
all the colors of the rainbow—
simple, elegant, one of a kind.

Promise

Early spring pops up
all of a sudden today,
dances me across the pasture,
twirls me high as robins in flight
then settles me down
in a field of daffodils and cherry
trees almost pink with bloom.

A cool breeze rustles my hair,
shakes out rusted worries,
softens, anchors me
to this land that feeds me.

A decision festers,
gathers force, commands
my full attention.
I shed my jacket,
sit on three tufts of tender
new turf in a warm spot
under clear afternoon sun,
slowly empty my mind.

One hawk watches from a wire
high as heaven.

Eden

I need these days at home,
all day long, unpresentable,
unseen by human eye.
The world stops while I hide
here in this garden.

Weeds know my ire.
The snake under a rock
detects my presence.

Birds call my name.
Grass grows under foot.
Butterflies sing
in tongues unknown.
A maple tree gives me shade
till shadows fall.

I have plans with the moon
after the sun is done with me.

Acknowledgments

Grateful acknowledgment is given to the following publications in which these poems originally appeared, some in earlier versions.

Creations Magazine: "Alacrity"
Freeing Jonah IV: "Jack Hall Remembered"
FutureCycle: "To My Only Child," "Born to Walk"
Journal of Kentucky Studies: "Sleepless," "Pick Flowers,"
    "Back to the Campfire"
Kentucky Review: "Absent," Pruning Time"
Red Fox Run: "Salvage," "Midsummer Night," "Mother"
Wild Goose Poetry Review: "Done In," "Building the House on
    Hanging Dog Creek," "Lunar Magic"

"At Leatherwood Falls" and "Eden" received Silver Arts Medals in the Cherokee County, North Carolina, Senior Games.

"Lost in the Roar of Big Santeetlah" took First Place in the Joyce Kilmer Memorial Forest 75th Anniversary National Poetry Contest (2011).

"Garden," "Manifesto," "Fireflies," "Sunday, Seven A.M.," "Flight," "I Knew," "Community Men," "The Counselor," "Counsel for Myself," "At Joyce Kilmer Forest," "I Hear the River Call My Name," and "At Home on Hanging Dog Creek" first appeared in the chapbook *I Hear the River Call My Name* (Finishing Line Press, 2007).

Cover artwork, "Tree Papier 12," by Billy Alexander; author photo by Wanda Willis; cover and interior book design by Diane Kistner; Didot text and titling

About FutureCycle Press

FutureCycle Press is dedicated to publishing lasting English-language poetry books, chapbooks, and anthologies in both print-on-demand and ebook formats. Founded in 2007 by long-time independent editor/publishers and partners Diane Kistner and Robert S. King, the press incorporated as a nonprofit in 2012. A number of our editors are distinguished poets and writers in their own right, and we have been actively involved in the small press movement going back to the early seventies.

The ˉFutureCycle Poetry Book Prize and honorarium is awarded annually for the best full-length volume of poetry we publish in a calendar year. Introduced in 2013, our Good Works projects are anthologies devoted to issues of universal significance, with all proceeds donated to a related worthy cause. Our Selected Poems series highlights contemporary poets with a substantial body of work to their credit; with this series we strive to resurrect work that has had limited distribution and is now out of print.

We are dedicated to giving all of the authors we publish the care their work deserves, making our catalog of titles the most diverse and distinguished it can be, and paying forward any earnings to fund more great books.

We've learned a few things about independent publishing over the years. We've also evolved a unique, resilient publishing model that allows us to focus mainly on vetting and preserving for posterity the most books of exceptional quality without becoming overwhelmed with bookkeeping and mailing, fundraising activities, or taxing editorial and production "bubbles." To find out more, come see us at www.futurecycle.org.

The FutureCycle Poetry Book Prize

All full-length volumes of poetry published by FutureCycle Press in any given calendar year are considered for the annual FutureCycle Poetry Book Prize. This allows us to consider each submission on its own merits, outside of the context of a contest. Too, the judges see the finished book, which will have benefitted from the beautiful book design and strong editorial gloss we are famous for.

The book ranked the best in judging is announced as the prize-winner in the subsequent year. There is no fixed monetary award; instead, the winning poet receives an honorarium of 20% of the total net royalties from all poetry books and chapbooks the press sold online in the year the winning book was published. The winner is also accorded the honor of being on the panel of judges for the next year's competition; all judges receive copies of all contending books to keep for their personal library.

www.ingramcontent.com/pod-product-compliance
Lightning Source LLC
Chambersburg PA
CBHW070010100426
42741CB00012B/3176